A Boy Called Slow

THE TRUE STORY OF SITTING BULL

JOSEPH BRUCHAC

ILLUSTRATED BY ROCCO BAVIERA

The Putnam & Grosset Group

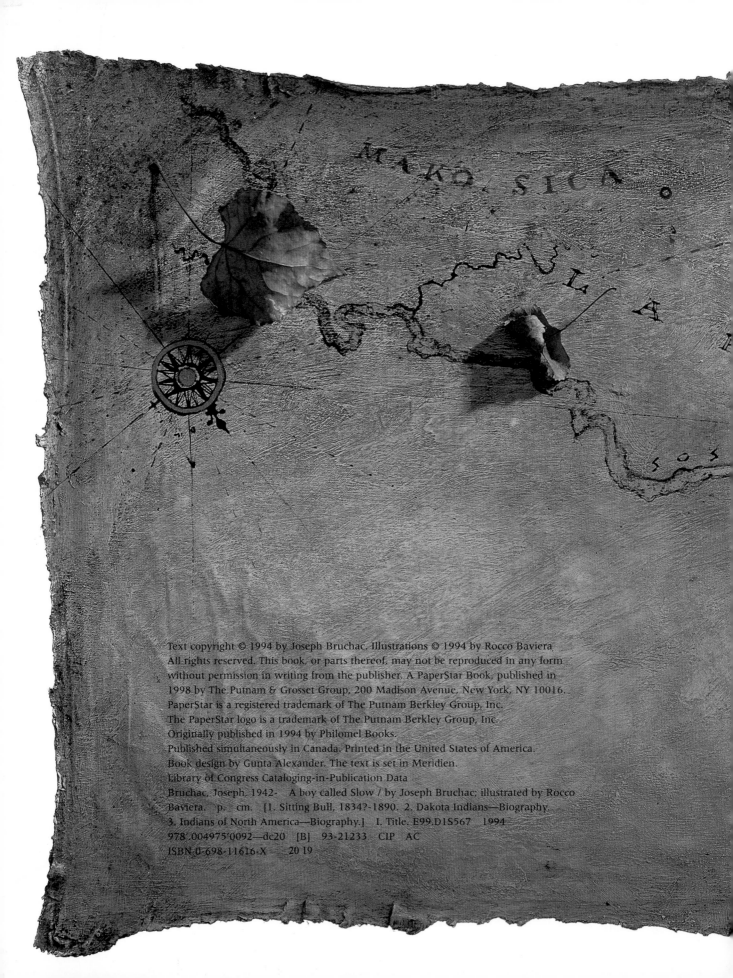

Text copyright © 1994 by Joseph Bruchac. Illustrations © 1994 by Rocco Baviera
A PaperStar Book, published in
1998 by The Putnam & Grosset Group, 200 Madison Avenue, New York, NY 10016.
PaperStar is a registered trademark of The Putnam Berkley Group, Inc.
The PaperStar logo is a trademark of The Putnam Berkley Group, Inc.
Originally published in 1994 by Philomel Books.
Published simultaneously in Canada. Printed in the United States of America.
Book design by Gunta Alexander. The text is set in Meridien.
Library of Congress Cataloging-in-Publication Data
Bruchac, Joseph. 1942-   A boy called Slow / by Joseph Bruchac; illustrated by Rocco
Baviera.   p.   cm.   [1. Sitting Bull, 1834?-1890. 2. Dakota Indians—Biography.
3. Indians of North America—Biography.]   I. Title. E99.D1S567   1994
978'.004975'0092—dc20   [B]   93-21233   CIP   AC
ISBN 0-698-11616-X   20 19

For my Grandfathers—J. B.

To the spirit of the Lakota people.—R. B.

Many years ago, in the winter of 1831,
a boy was born to the family of Returns Again
of the Hunkpapa band of the Lakota Sioux.

Though Returns Again loved his daughters—knowing well that women are the heart of the nation—both he and his wife gave thanks to Wakan-Tanka for at last giving them a son.

"Now," Returns Again said, "we have one who will hunt for his Hunkpapa people and help to protect them."

But his wife smiled. *"Han!"* she said. "We have one to follow his father's path."

It was the custom in those days to give a childhood name. Such names came from the way a child acted. So it had been with Returns Again and his father before him.

So the parents of this boy and the other relatives in his *tiyospaye,* his extended family, watched the first son of Returns Again closely.

If he had tried to swallow everything he could get hold of—as was the case with one of his cousins—they might have called him "Hungry Mouth." But that was not so for this boy.

"If he were to take much longer eating," his uncle Four Horns said, "the food would bite him before he bites it!"

Perhaps, his mother thought, if he were quick in his movements and always watching things they might call him "Mouse." But that was not the case for this boy. He never did anything quickly. This son of Returns Again was always slow.

"*U we!*" his mother said. "Come here, quickly!" But her son only looked at her.

"*Nihwa hwo?*" Returns Again would say. "Are you sleepy?" But it was not sleep that made their son act as he did. It was simply the way he was. Every action he took was slow.

"*Slon-he,*" his father said. "That is the name for our son."

His mother agreed. "We will call him Slow."

So that became his name.

Slow's uncle Four Horns would tell Slow how the horses came to the plains only in the time of Slow's grandparents, and how the horses made their lives easier than they had been in the old days. Some said that the horses were brought by the *wasicun*, the white man. But Four Horns told him a different story.

"Our Creator, Wakan-Tanka, loves the Lakota people," his uncle would tell him. "Wakan-Tanka saw that we had only our dogs to help us pull our travois and hunt buffalo. So Wakan-Tanka sent us a new animal as faithful as our dogs but able to pull our loads and carry us as quick as the whirlwind into the hunt, the *Shoong-Ton'kah*, the 'Spirit Dog.'"

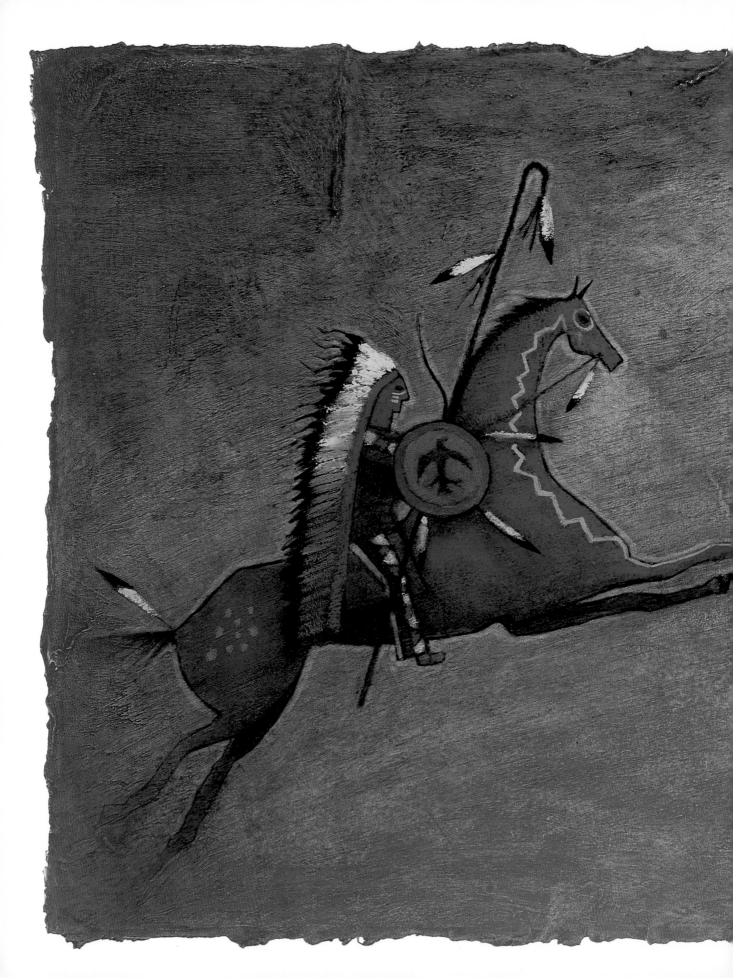

As Slow grew up, he was not happy with his name. Few
boys were given names they wanted to keep. No one wanted
to be known as "Hungry Mouth" or "Curly" or "Runny Nose"
or "Slow" all of his life. But until a child earned a new name
by having a powerful dream or by doing some brave or
special deed, it could not be changed.

Slow wished for this vision of bravery to come to him. He
wished for a vision that would allow him to prove himself to
his people.

Slow longed to have a name like his uncle Four Horns, or like the strong name his father had earned—Returns Again to Strike the Enemy.

"Your father," Slow's mother said, "was given his name because of his courage in battle. When the Crows raided our village, the others were ready to retreat, but your father was the one who returned. Because of his bravery, the enemies were driven away. "You must always help and protect your people," she continued. "A true Lakota shares everything with the people."

Slow listened to his mother's words, knowing how true they were. He had often seen his father return from hunting and share what he brought back with the poorest people in the village. He remembered two winters ago when his father returned from a raid and brought back many horses. Returns Again had given all of those horses away except for one strong gray pony, which he saved for his son.

"The best way," Returns Again told him, "to gain the respect of your people is to be both brave and wise."

Slow understood those words. By the time Slow reached his seventh winter, he had gained a reputation as one of the strongest of the boys. And when it came to riding, none of the small children was more at ease on the back of a pony than the boy called Slow.

Returns Again was a man who could sometimes understand the speech of the animals and the birds. Slow, too, inherited some of his father's gift. He knew that his gray pony understood him, and when he was on its back, it was as if the two of them were one. Slow knew that many of his Lakota people

could speak with the birds and animals, and hear their speech
as clearly as human words; and the animals understood them,
as well. And because he listened to the animals, Returns Again
was given four more names.

One summer, Returns Again went hunting with some friends. As they camped at night beside their fire not far from the place called Smoky Butte, they heard a sound approaching them. It was a low sound, like a deep voice talking. Someone was coming along the trail which led between the low hills. The other men reached for their weapons, but Returns Again stopped them. There, coming slowly along the trail toward them, was a big bull buffalo, its head close to the ground. The deep murmuring sound came from its throat. The other men could not make out what the buffalo was saying, but Returns Again heard it clearly. Returns Again listened carefully as the buffalo spoke, for the words it spoke were names:

> *Tatan'ka Iyota'ke,*
> *Tatan'ka Psi'ca,*
> *Tatan'ka Winyu'ha Najin,*
> *Tatan'ka Wanji'la*

Those were the four names spoken by the great bull buffalo. They were powerful names. As the buffalo slowly passed them and continued on along the trail until it was over the hill and out of sight, Returns Again knew that those names had been given to him. From that day on, he owned not only the name Returns Again to Strike the Enemy, he also owned those four names given him by the old bull buffalo.

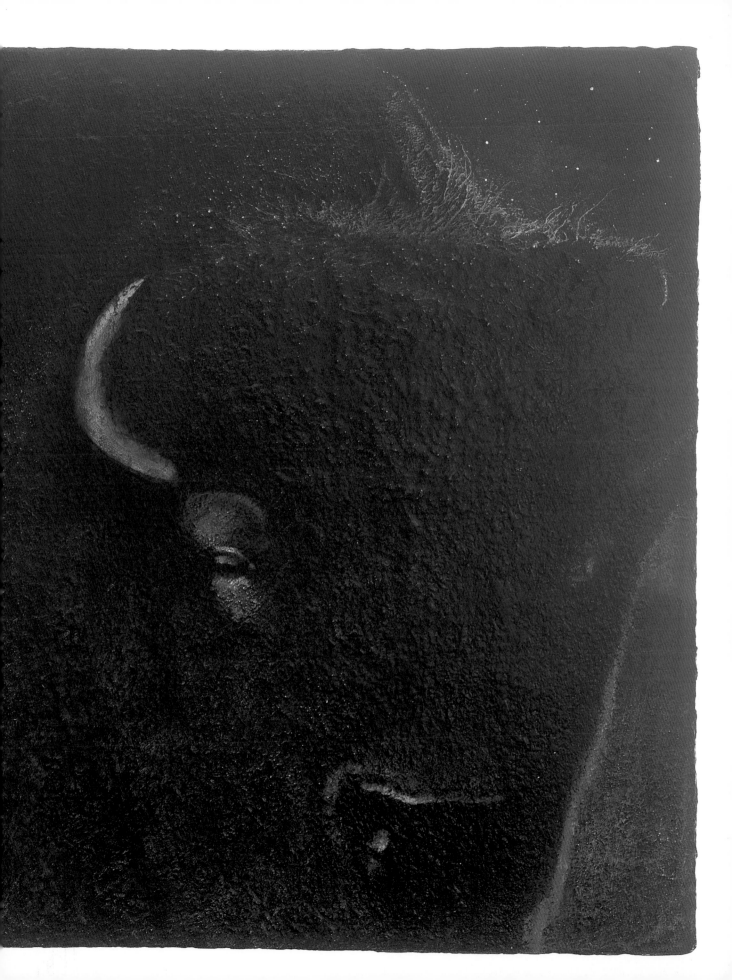

Slow was proud to have a father with such names as
Returns Again and Tatan'ka Iyota'ke. One day, he promised
himself, he too would have such a strong name. But he knew
that it would not be easy. So, as Slow wrestled with his
friends, as he hunted with his bow and arrows, as he raced
his gray pony, he always tried to do his best so that one day
he would become a good warrior.

Slow was careful and deliberate in everything he did. It

might take him a while to decide, but once he put his head down and went forward, he would not turn back.

At the age of ten, he killed his first buffalo—a yearling calf. His mother skinned the buffalo calf and, with his two sisters helping, tanned its skin and made it into a robe for him to wear. Though he was still called Slow, no one teased him any longer. His name now meant determination and courage to those who knew him.

As the winters passed, Slow grew. He was not as tall as some of the boys his age, but his shoulders were broad and strong.

One evening, he heard word in the camp that his father and some other men were going to ride out against the Crow, who his father called his favorite enemies. Slow knew that the Crow were great warriors and had some of the best horses on the plains. Slow had now seen fourteen winters and was old enough to go along.

He wrapped his robe made of the skin of the buffalo calf around his shoulders. He picked up his bow and his quiver full of blunt-pointed arrows that he used for hunting birds. He quickly brushed his gray pony's tail and plucked a burr from its mane. *"Mitakola,"* he said, *"*my friend, we are ready to help protect the people."

Determined, he rode through the cottonwood trees until he reached the trail his father's war party had taken. Before long, Slow came to the place where they had chosen to gather and make plans. He rode into their midst and before his father or any of the other men could speak, he jumped from his pony's back and put his arm over the animal's neck.

"We are going," Slow said.

Returns Again looked around at the other men and then looked at his son with pride.

"*Han*," he said.

The war party began to ride to the place where the Red River meets the Missouri River.

When at last they were close to the place, the men who had been sent ahead as scouts came back.

"*Upelo*," the scouts said. "They are coming!"

The men began to make preparations. They put on their best clothing and brought out their paint to mark their faces and their horses. They uncovered their war shields and took out their coup sticks and their lances. From behind a small hill, they had a good view of the plain before them and could see the enemy coming from a long way off.

Closer and closer the enemy came, ready for attack.

Everyone waited for Slow's father to give the word. But
as he waited, Slow's father looked over to his right. There,
already mounted on his horse, was Slow. All that he wore
were his moccasins and his breech cloth and he held a coup
stick in his hand. He looked over at his father and then he
kicked his horse's sides.

"Hiyu'wo!" the boy shouted. His horse leaped forward and
over the top of the hill, down toward the enemy. His father
and the rest of the war party tried to catch up, but Slow's
horse was too far ahead.

The Crow war party at the base of the hill looked up to see many men galloping down.

One of the Crow warriors drew an arrow to his bowstring, but before he could let it go, Slow had reached him and struck his arm with the coup stick, spoiling his aim. *"Oh-hey,"* Slow cried in triumph.

At the sight of Slow and the men, the Crow warriors fled.
"Hiyu'wo, Hiyu'wo!"

When the fight was over, not one Hunkpapa warrior had
been injured. The Lakota people brought back many horses
and weapons from the Crow. The raid was a success.

Slow was a hero.

When they returned to their village, all of the men spoke in loud voices of the brave deeds they had done. But the loudest voice of all was the voice of Slow's father. He painted his son with black paint—a sign of his victory.

"My son is brave," he said. "His determination has won the battle for us. I give him a new name. I give him the name that was mine. He is no longer *Slon-he*. He is now *Tatan'ka Iyota'ke*."

And so it was that the boy who was once called "Slow" gained the name *Tatan'ka Iyota'ke*, a name which is known well, for *Tatan'ka Iyota'ke* means Sitting Bull—one of the greatest of all the Lakota warriors.

And this is his story.